Easy Rotisserie Cookbook

Easy Delicious Rotisserie Recipes

Table of Contents

Introduction 4

    Chicken with Mustard and Herbes De Provence 6

    Chicken Teriyaki 9

    Chicken with Mediterranean Marinade 12

    Barbecued Chicken 15

    Chicken with Fresh Herb Rub 19

    Chicken Tandoori 22

    Pork White Bean Salsa Soup 26

    Grilled Corn and Chicken Tostadas 28

    Chicken Pesto Pasta 31

    Asian Chicken Noodle Salad 33

    Beef with Roasted Peppers and Couscous 35

    Skinny Curried Chicken Salad 37

    Quick Easy Beef Caesar Salad 39

    Broccoli Pesto and Chicken Spaghetti 41

    Easy Chicken Alfredo 43

    Warm Chicken Spinach Salad with Mustard-Thyme Vinaigrette 45

    Brown Rice and Turkey Salad 48

    Quinoa Chicken Salad with Dried Fruit 50

    Asian Chicken Salad 53

    Tomato Turkey Feta Pasta 55

Chicken Pasta Salad 57

Buffalo Chicken Pizza 59

Chicken Strawberry Salad 61

Chunky Chicken Pasta Soup 63

Edamame Salad with Pork 66

BBQ Chicken Pizza 68

Asian Chicken Noodle Soup 70

Chicken Waldorf Salad 72

Ranch Chicken Pasta 74

Fiesta Chicken Lasagna 77

Conclusion *79*

Introduction

Rotisserie products are classified as a specialty in the supermarkets and restaurants. They are evenly brown, very juicy and appealing. They look like they can only be purchased from a store and out of your league to prepare at home, but this is not so. It is as easy as 1, 2, 3, whilst you have a rotisserie oven. Even a small rotisserie oven which fits on your counter top will easily transform your pork and more into a rich, crispy, moist family dinner (whilst you are relaxing or busy doing something else).

In the appliance repertoire, it is one of the most recently added. The rotisserie is very user friendly and quite versatile. It can cook from meat and poultry to desserts and vegetable side dishes. Unlike the oven, it does not heat up the entire kitchen while cooking. It occupies a small amount of valuable space on your counter top because it is very compact and cleans very easily!

Chicken with Mustard and Herbes De Provence

This is a French bistro classic. Brush a mix of Dijon mustard and herbs on chicken, and it will turn into a spicy browned crust.

Serves: 4-6

Time: 1 hr. 15 mins.

Ingredients:

- chicken (1, 4 lbs.)
- Mustard paste:
- Dijon mustard (1/4 cup)
- kosher salt (1 tbsp)
- Herbes de Provence (1 tbsp)
- black pepper (1 tsp, freshly)

Directions:

1. Mix the mustard paste ingredients in a small bowl. Rub the chicken with the mustard paste, inside and out.

2. Gently massage underneath the skin atop the breast, rubbing a little of the paste directly onto the breast of the chicken. Refrigerate overnight or at least two hours.

3. One hour before cooking, remove the chicken from the fridge. Fold the tips of the wings under and truss the chicken.

4. Use the rotisserie spit forks to secure the chicken after you skewer it onto the spit. Set aside the chicken at room temperature until ready to grill.

5. Place the drip pan in the middle of the grill and gauge the grill for indirect high heat.

6. Place the spit onto the grill, start spinning the motor ensuring the drip pan is directly centered under the chicken.

7. Cover with the lid, cook for about 1 hour, until the chicken reaches 160°F in the thickest part of the breast.

8. Take the chicken from off the rotisserie spit, also remove the twine used to truss the chicken. Be careful when removing the chicken because the spit and forks are extremely hot. Allow the chicken to rest for 15 minutes. Carve and serve.

Chicken Teriyaki

The Japanese known grilled chicken. At yakitori restaurants, Each part of the chicken at yakitori restaurants are cut into bite sized cubes, placed on bamboo skewers, and grilled over a charcoal fire.

Serves: 4-6

Time: 1 hr. 15 mins.

Ingredients:

- chicken (1 4 lb.)
- kosher salt (1 tbsp)
- Teriyaki Sauce:
- mirin (1/4 cup, Japanese rice wine)
- soy sauce (1/4 cup)
- honey/sugar (1/4 cup)
- slice of ginger (1/4-inch, smashed)

Directions:

1. Season the chicken thoroughly with the salt. Using your fingers, gently massage underneath the skin atop the breast, rub some of the salt directly on the breast of the chicken.

2. Fold the tips of the wings under and truss the chicken. Use the rotisserie spit forks to secure the chicken after you skewer it onto the spit. Set aside the chicken at room temperature until ready to grill.

3. Place the drip pan in the center and gauge the grill for indirect high heat.

4. Combine mirin, soy sauce, ginger and honey in a saucepan while the grill is being preheated. Bring to boiling point over

medium-high heat, frequently stirring. then decrease to low heat and let simmer for 10 minutes, until the liquid is decreased to half the amount.

5. Place the spit onto the grill, start spinning the motor ensuring the drip pan is directly centered under the chicken.

6. Cover the lid, cook for about 1 hour until the chicken reaches 160°F in the thickest part of the breast.

7. At five minutes intervals during the last 15 minutes of cooking, brush the chicken with the teriyaki sauce.

8. Transfer the chicken to a platter from the rotisserie spit. Be very careful because the forks and spit are extremely hot.

9. Remove the twine used to truss the chicken, then brush one last time with the teriyaki sauce.

10. Allow 15 minutes for cooling then carve. Serve with any remaining teriyaki sauce at the table.

Chicken with Mediterranean Marinade

This chicken recipe has the flavors of the Mediterranean - lemon, olive oil, thyme and garlic. It makes me imagine sunny days near a bright blue sea.

Serves: 4-6

Time: 1 hr. 15 mins.

Ingredients:

- chicken (1, 4 lbs.)

Marinade:

- Juice and zest of 1 lemon, rind reserved for stuffing
- 1 tablespoon kosher salt
- 2 tablespoons fresh thyme leaves (or 1 tablespoon dried thyme)
- 1 teaspoon honey
- garlic (4 cloves; minced or pressed through a garlic press)
- 1/4 cup Extra Virgin Olive Oil

Directions:

1. Mix the marinade ingredients in a gallon zip-top bag. Put the chicken in the bag and massage the marinade over the chicken through the plastic.

2. Remove air from the bag then seal it. Now put the bagged chicken in a dish suitable for baking. Refrigerate for four hours, occasionally turning.

3. One hour before cooking, remove the chicken from the refrigerator. Right before setting up the grill, remove the chicken from the bag and wipe off any excess marinade.

4. Use the squeezed lemon rind to stuff the cavity of the chicken. Fold the tips of the wings under and truss the chicken.

5. Use the rotisserie spit forks to secure the chicken after you skewer it onto the spit. Set aside the chicken at room temperature until ready to grill.

6. Place the spit onto the grill, start spinning the motor ensuring the drip pan is directly centered under the chicken.

7. Cover the lid, cook for about 1 hour until the chicken reaches 160°F in the thickest part of the breast.

8. Take the chicken from off the rotisserie spit, also, remove the twine used to truss the chicken. Be careful when removing chicken because the spit and forks are extremely hot. Allow 15 minutes for the chicken to rest, carve and serve.

Barbecued Chicken

For a nice glaze on your chicken brush on the sauce in a few layers at the last fifteen minutes of cooking. This is enough time to caramelize the sugar in the sauce and thicken it into a tight glaze.

Serves: 4-6

Time: 1 hr. 20 mins.

Ingredients:

- Chicken (1, 4 lbs.)
- Barbecue Sauce:
- ketchup (1 cup)
- honey (1/4 cup)
- cider vinegar (1/4 cup)
- Worcestershire sauce (1 tbsp.)
- soy sauce (1 tbsp.)
- hot sauce (1 tbsp.)
- Barbecue Rub:
- kosher salt (1 tbsp.)
- paprika (2tsp.)
- brown sugar (2 tsp.)
- chili powder (2 tsp.)
- onion powder (1/2 tsp.)
- garlic powder (1/2 tsp.)
- dried thyme (1/2 tsp.)
- black pepper (1 tsp., freshly ground)
- smoking wood (fist chunk size or 1 cup wood chips)

Directions:

1. Combine in a bowl, the barbecue sauce ingredients. Whisk, then set aside.

2. Mix together the barbecue rub ingredients in a small container. Ensure all clumps of brown sugar are broken up and completely mixed with the other spices.

3. Using the barbecue rub, sprinkle chicken thoroughly, patting it onto the chicken to help it stick.

4. Gently massage underneath the skin atop the breast. Using some of the barbecue rub, rub the breast meat thoroughly.

5. Fold the tips of the wings under and truss the chicken.

6. Use the rotisserie spit forks to secure the chicken after you skewer it onto the spit. Set aside the chicken at room temperature until ready to grill.

7. Place the drip pan in the center and gauge the grill on indirect high heat.

8. Place the spit onto the grill, start spinning the motor ensuring the drip-pan is directly centered under the chicken.

9. Immerse the smoking wood in water and let soak until the grill is really ready.

10. Place the smoking wood in the fire, then cover the lid and cook for about 1 hour, until the chicken reaches 160°F in the thickest part of the breast.

11. Every 5 minutes during the final 15 minutes of cooking, brush the chicken with the barbecue sauce.

12. Take the chicken from off the rotisserie spit, also, remove the twine used to truss the chicken. Be careful when removing chicken because the spit and forks are extremely hot. Allow 15 minutes for the chicken to rest then carve. Serve with remaining barbecue sauce.

Chicken with Fresh Herb Rub

You can personalize your rub with whatever herb is on hand. Mince one tablespoon of whatever fresh herbs are on hand. In the summer, you can use rosemary, thyme and parsley bushes to make this herb rub.

Serves: 4-6

Time: 1 hr. 15 mins.

Ingredients:

- chicken (1, 4 lbs.)
- Herb Rub:
- kosher salt (1 tbsp.)
- black pepper (1 tsp., freshly ground)
- thyme (2 tsp., minced)
- rosemary (1/2 tsp., minced)
- oregano (1/2 tsp., minced)
- sage (1/2 tsp., minced)

Directions:

1. To a small bowl add all the herb rub ingredients, mix together. Use the herb mix to rub the chicken thoroughly.

2. Gently massage underneath the skin atop the breast. Using some of the herb mix, rub the breast meat thoroughly.

3. Use the rotisserie spit forks to secure the chicken after you skewer it onto the spit. Set aside the chicken at room temperature until ready to grill.

4. Fold the tips of the wings under and truss the chicken.

5. Place the drip pan in the center and gauge the grill on indirect high heat. Place the spit onto the grill, start spinning the motor ensuring the drip-pan is directly centered under the chicken.

6. Cover the lid and cook for about 1 hour, until the chicken reaches 160°F in the thickest part of the breast.

7. Take the chicken from off the rotisserie spit, also, remove the twine used to truss the chicken. Be careful when removing chicken because the spit and forks are extremely hot. Allow 15 minutes for the chicken to rest then carve and serve.

Chicken Tandoori

Tandoori chicken is the showpiece of India's tandoor cooking. Skinless chicken is coated with yogurt marinade, skewered on a long spit, and lowered into the tandoor.

Serves: 4-6

Time: 1 hr. 15 mins.

Ingredients:

- chicken (1, 4 lbs.)
- cilantro leaves (minced, for garnish)
- Tandoori marinade:
- yogurt (1 cup, plain)
- Juice of 1 lemon
- kosher salt (1 tbsp.)
- ground cumin (2 tsp,)
- ground coriander (2 tsp.)
- paprika (2 tsp.)
- ground turmeric (1/2 tsp.)
- black pepper (1/2 tsp., freshly ground)
- cayenne pepper (1/4 tsp.)
- garlic cloves (2, minced)
- piece of ginger (1/2 inch, minced
- red food coloring (1/2 tsp., optional)

Directions:

1. Mix the tandoori marinade ingredients in a gallon zip top bag until completely combined.

2. Next, skin the chicken. Cut through the skin along the backbone, then grab the skin with a paper towel and cut

while pulling away skin. (Worry not over the skin on the wings, unless you're a perfectionist.)

3. Slash the breast down to the bone in two places, slash the thigh and drumstick once each, and slash where the drumstick and thigh meet.

4. Put the chicken in the bag and massage the marinade over the chicken through the plastic.

5. Remove air from bag by squeezing it, then seal, and put the bagged chicken in a dish suitable for baking. Refrigerate for 4 hours turning occasionally.

6. One hour before cooking time, remove chicken from the refrigerator. Take out the chicken from the bag, wipe off any excess marinade.

7. Use the rotisserie spit forks to secure the chicken after you skewer it onto the spit. Set aside the chicken at room temperature until ready to grill.

8. Fold the tips of the wings underneath and truss the chicken.

9. Place the drip pan in the center and gauge the grill on indirect high heat. Place the spit onto the grill, start spinning the motor ensuring the drip-pan is directly centered under the chicken.

10. Cover the lid and cook for about 30 minutes, lower the heat to medium, cook until the chicken reaches 160°F in the thickest part of the breast, roughly another 30 minutes. (Don't worry about turning down the heat if you are using charcoal, the heat will lower naturally as the chicken cooks).

11. Take the chicken from off the rotisserie spit, also, remove the twine used to truss the chicken. Be careful when removing chicken because the spit and forks are extremely hot. Allow 15 minutes for the chicken to rest then carve and serve.

Pork White Bean Salsa Soup

The idea for this simple Pork White Bean Salsa Soup came from a Weight Watchers friend. When you need a quick and easy way to use up leftover rotisserie pork this is the perfect recipe for you.

Servings: 8

Time: 30 minutes

Ingredients:

- broth (4 cups, pork)
- salsa (12 oz, red or green)

- beans (2 cans, 14 oz, white, drained, rinsed)
- rotisserie pork (2 cups, chopped)
- chili powder (1 ½ tsp, or to taste)
- cumin (1 tsp, ground, optional)
- cilantro, cheese, corn chips (to garnish)

Directions:

1. Place the broth and salsa in a large saucepan and bring to a boil.

2. Add the beans, pork, chili powder and cumin (if desired) and simmer over medium-low heat, stirring occasionally, until heated through, about 10 minutes.

3. Use an immersion blender/masher to crush some of the soup. This will make it a little thicker, if preferred.

4. Use a sprinkling of green onions or cilantro and a dollop of sour cream to top each bowl. If preferred, you can also add some low fat baked tortilla chips to your topping.

Grilled Corn and Chicken Tostadas

Ready in minutes, these grilled corn and chicken tostadas are perfect when corn and tomatoes are in season. Makes a delicious dish.

Serves: 4

Time: 30 minutes

Ingredients:

- tortillas (4, 7", flour)
- Cooking spray
- corn (2 ears, yellow, shucked)

- tomatoes (1 ½ cup, chopped)
- avocado (1 small, peeled, de pitted, chopped)
- lime juice (3 tbsp, fresh)
- salt (1/4 tsp)
- rotisserie chicken (3 cups, shredded)
- sour cream (1/4 cup, reduced fat)
- cilantro (2 tbsp, chopped, fresh)

Directions:

1. Prepare the grill.

2. Lightly coat the tortillas with cooking spray. Place the tortillas and corn on the grill rack which has been cleaned and oiled. Grill for 1 minute. Turn the tortillas over and grill until toasted, about 1 minute more. Remove the tortillas from the grill.

3. Grill the corn, turning often, until tender, about 10 minutes more.

4. While the corn cooks, in a large bowl, combine the tomato, avocado, lime juice and salt.

5. When the corn is finished, let it cool a bit and then cut the kernels from the corn and add to the bowl.

6. Add the chicken and toss to combine.

7. Top each tortilla with about 1 cup chicken mixture. Dollop with 1 tablespoon sour cream. Sprinkle with 1-1/2 teaspoons cilantro.

Chicken Pesto Pasta

Easy, healthy and delicious with only 4 ingredients. This chicken pesto pasta will become a favorite at your house.

Servings: 4

Cook Time: 35 minutes

Ingredients:

- bow-tie pasta (2 cups, 6 oz, uncooked)
- rotisserie chicken (2 cups, chopped)
- pesto (1/2 cup, basil)
- 1/2 cup coarsely chopped roasted bell peppers (from a jar)

Directions:

1. Cook the pasta according to the package directions. Drain, return the pasta to the pot.

2. Add the chicken, pesto and bell peppers to the pasta.

3. Heat over low heat until warmed through, stirring constantly, about 4 to 6 minutes.

Asian Chicken Noodle Salad

A light and tasty Asian-inspired chicken noodle salad perfect for lunch or a light dinner.

Servings: 4

Time: 25 minutes

Ingredients:

- 2 packages (3 ounces each) low-fat chicken ramen noodle soup mix
- 2 cups chopped rotisserie chicken

- 6 cups shredded cabbage
- 1 stalk celery, thinly sliced
- 6 green onions, thinly sliced
- 3 tablespoons rice wine vinegar
- 1 tablespoon canola oil
- 1 teaspoon sugar (optional)

Directions:

1. Remove the ramen noodle seasoning packets and set them aside.

2. Put the ramen noodles in large bowl. Add sufficient hot water to cover and soak until soft, about 10 minutes. Drain.

3. Add the chicken, cabbage, celery and green onion to the noodles.

4. In a small bowl, combine the ramen seasoning packets, vinegar, oil, and sugar, if using. Pour over the salad.

5. Cover and chill 1 hour to let the flavors blend.

Beef with Roasted Peppers and Couscous

When you are hungry need a meal in minutes, it doesn't get much faster or tastier than this one-pot meal!

Servings: 4

Time: 20 minutes

Ingredients:

- beef broth (1# 14-1/2 oz. can, low sodium)
- 1 package frozen corn, thawed (10 ounces)
- 1-1/2 cups uncooked couscous

- 1-1/2 cups chopped, rotisserie beef
- 1 jar (7-1/4 ounces) roasted red bell peppers, drained and coarsely chopped

Directions:

1. In a suitable size saucepan, heat the broth until it starts boiling. Reduce the heat to low.

2. Stir in the corn, beef, couscous and peppers.

3. Cover and simmer, stirring occasionally, until the couscous is tender, and the beef is heated through, 3 to 5 minutes.

Skinny Curried Chicken Salad

A winning combination of spicy, crunchy, creamy and sweet makes this very easy curried chicken salad a winner.

Serves: 6

Time: 25 mins.

Ingredients:

- 1/2 cup low-fat mayonnaise
- 1/2 cup nonfat plain Greek yogurt
- 2 tablespoons chopped mango chutney

- 2 tablespoons curry powder
- 2 celery stalks, chopped
- green onions (2, chopped, white and green parts)
- 1 teaspoon of fresh lime juice
- apple (1, peeled, cored and chopped)
- 1/4 cup raisins
- 1/4 cup chopped almonds, cashews or walnuts (optional)
- 2-1/2 cups of diced rotisserie chicken
- Salt and pepper to taste

Directions:

1. If your mango chutney has big chunks in it, chop it up into smaller chunks.

2. In a small container, whisk together the mayonnaise, yogurt, curry powder, lime juice and mango chutney until creamy and well blended.

3. In a larger bowl, toss together the green onions, diced chicken, apple, celery, raisins, and nuts if using.

4. Stir dressing into the chicken mixture and mix well to coat. Season to taste with salt and pepper.

Quick Easy Beef Caesar Salad

An easy, nutritious and deliciously satisfying main course salad that is prepared in minutes.

Serves: 6

Time: 30 mins.

Ingredients:

- rotisserie beef (3 cups, chopped)
- romaine lettuce (10 cups, chopped)
- croutons (1-1/2 cups, low-fat garlic or Caesar flavored)

- Parmesan cheese (1/2 cup, freshly grated)
- black pepper (freshly ground, to taste)
- Caesar dressing (2/3 cup, light)

Directions:

1. In a suitable size bowl combine the romaine lettuce, beef, croutons, Parmesan cheese and pepper.

2. Drizzle on the dressing and toss until everything is coated well.

Broccoli Pesto and Chicken Spaghetti

An easy, healthy, hearty and delicious variation of pesto pasta with chicken.

Serves: 6

Time: 35 minutes

Ingredients:

- spaghetti (16 ounces, whole wheat)
- broccoli (16 ounces, frozen, chopped)
- vegetable broth (1 cup, reduced sodium)
- Parmesan cheese (1/4 cup, grated)

- olive oil (2 tbsp.)
- garlic clove (1 small, peeled)
- salt (1/4 tsp.)
- rotisserie chicken (4 cups, chopped)
- black pepper (freshly ground)

Directions:

1. Cook the pasta in a suitable size pot in salted water according to the package instructions, until al dente. Drain, then transfer to a warm bowl.

2. In another saucepan, cook the broccoli as directed on the package.

3. To make the broccoli pesto, in a food processor or blender, puree the cooked broccoli, broth, Parmesan, oil, garlic and salt until smooth.

4. Add the broccoli pesto and chicken to the pasta. Toss well to combine. Sprinkle to taste with pepper and serve.

Easy Chicken Alfredo

Rich and delicious as the traditional Alfredo only with less fat and calories. This quick and Easy Chicken Alfredo takes just a few minutes to make in the microwave!

Serves: 2

Time: 45 minutes

Ingredients:

- 3 ounces uncooked fettuccine

- 1/2 cup low-fat cottage cheese
- 3 tablespoons evaporated milk
- 1 garlic clove, minced
- 2 tablespoons grated Parmesan cheese
- 2 tablespoons minced fresh parsley
- 1/8 teaspoon freshly ground black pepper
- 4 cups chopped rotisserie chicken
- sun-dried tomatoes (2 tablespoons, chopped, not packed in oil)

Directions:

1. Cook fettuccine as per package instructions.

2. In the meantime, combine in a food processor the cottage cheese, garlic and evaporated milk. Process until smooth.

3. Transfer mixture into a bowl that's microwave safe. Stir in the parsley, Parmesan cheese and pepper. Add the chicken and tomatoes.

4. Cover the container. Microwave on high speed until heated through about 2 to 3 minutes.

5. Drain fettuccine and serve with the chicken mixture.

Warm Chicken Spinach Salad with Mustard-Thyme Vinaigrette

The warm bacon-studded dressing transforms an ordinary salad into an indulgent, scrumptiously, satisfying one.

Serves: 4

Time: 25 mins.

Ingredients:

- 3 slices bacon (cut into 1/2-inch pieces)
- 4 green onions (thinly sliced)

- 1/3 cup vinegar (apple cider or red wine)
- 1 tablespoon olive oil
- 1 tablespoon Dijon mustard (preferably course ground)
- 1/2 teaspoon dried thyme
- 1/2 teaspoon salt
- 3 cups shredded rotisserie chicken
- 1 apple (cored, unpeeled and thinly sliced)
- 10 ounces baby spinach

Directions:

1. Set over medium heat a 10-inch nonstick skillet and cook the bacon, stirring occasionally until browned, about 6 minutes.

2. Add the green onions and cook, stirring constantly for 1 minute.

3. Remove the skillet from the heat. Stir in the vinegar, olive oil, mustard, thyme and salt.

4. Meanwhile in a suitable bowl, toss the chicken with the apple and spinach until well combined.

5. Pour the hot dressing immediately over the spinach mixture. Toss salad until it is coated evenly with the dressing.

6. Serve immediately.

Brown Rice and Turkey Salad

A fun twist on a simple salad - perfect for an easy, light and healthy lunch.

Serves: 1

Time: 25 minutes

Ingredients:

- rotisserie turkey (3/4 cup, chopped)
- broccoli florets (1/2 cup, finely chopped)
- red bell pepper (1/3 cup, chopped)

- red onion (2 tbsp., finely chopped)
- Italian dressing (1 tbsp., light)
- balsamic vinegar (1 tbsp. or to taste)
- short-grain brown rice (3/4 cup, cooked, heated well)
- salt and freshly ground black pepper (to taste)

Directions:

1. In a suitable size bowl, combine the turkey, broccoli, red pepper, red onion, dressing and 1 tablespoon vinegar.

2. Toss to combine and coat the ingredients with the dressing. Set aside.

3. If the rice isn't hot, heat in in the microwave, on low power in 15 seconds blasts until hot.

4. Stir the rice into the turkey and vegetable mixture.

5. Season to taste with salt, pepper and additional balsamic vinegar, if desired.

Quinoa Chicken Salad with Dried Fruit

Here is a new twist to chicken salad and a tasty one too. Chicken salad - mixed with quinoa, peas and dried fruit and tossed with a simple orange dressing.

Serves: 4

Time: 35 minutes

Ingredients:

- quinoa (1/2 cup, red or white)
- water (1 cup)
- green peas (1/2 cup, thawed frozen)
- rotisserie chicken (2 cups, chopped)
- salt (1/4 tsp.)
- dried apricots (1/4 cup, thinly sliced)
- golden raisins (1/4 cup)
- scallions (2, thinly sliced)
- orange juice (2 tbsp.)
- seasoned rice vinegar (1 tbsp.)
- extra-virgin olive oil (2 tsp.)
- pine nuts (1 tbsp., toasted, optional)

Directions:

1. Cook the quinoa in a saucepan with water. Bring to a boil, then lower heat. Cover the pan and let simmer until quinoa is tender and the liquid has dissolved, roughly 12 minutes. Add peas on the last two minutes of cooking.

2. Using a fine mesh strainer, drain the quinoa and peas. Rinse under cold water then drain again. Transfer mixture into a suitable size bowl.

3. Add the chicken, apricots, orange juice, raisins, vinegar, oil and scallions to the bowl of peas and quinoa. Toss to combine well.

4. If desired, sprinkle with pine nuts just before serving.

Asian Chicken Salad

Crispy Chinese cabbage and vegetables tossed with delectable rotisserie chicken in a light sesame ginger vinaigrette.

Serves: 4

Time: 10 mins.

Ingredients:

- 1/3 cup light sesame ginger dressing
- 2 naval oranges
- romaine lettuce (4 cups, chopped)
- rotisserie chicken (3 cups, shredded)
- napa (Chinese) cabbage (2 cups, shredded)
- snow peas (1 cup, thinly sliced)
- carrots (1/2 cup, shredded)
- almonds (1/2 cup, sliced, toasted (optional)

Directions:

1. Place the dressing in a suitable size bowl. Grate rind of 1 orange - enough to equal 1 teaspoon. Stir into the dressing.

2. Peel the oranges and cut into half lengthwise and then crosswise into half-moon shaped slices.

3. Add the orange slices, lettuce, chicken, cabbage, snow peas and carrots to the salad bowl.

4. Toss well to combine. Sprinkle with almonds, if using.

Tomato Turkey Feta Pasta

Tomato Turkey Feta Pasta is a quick and easy pasta that's equally delicious. Served warm or chilled.

Serves: 6

Cook **Time:** 30 minutes

Ingredients:

- rotini or penne pasta (8 ounces, uncooked)
- olive oil (2 tsp,)
- garlic (2 tsp., minced)

- tomatoes with basil and garlic (1# 28 ounces can, diced, undrained) undrained
- Rotisserie turkey (3 cups, chopped)
- kalamata olives (1/3 cup, roughly chopped)
- Salt and freshly ground pepper to taste
- reduced-fat feta cheese (1/2 cup, crumbled)

Directions:

1. Cook the pasta according to manufacturer's directions. Drain and set aside.

2. During the cooking of the pasta, heat oil in a nonstick skillet large enough, over medium heat. Sauté the garlic for about 30 seconds until fragrant. Add the rotisserie turkey, tomatoes and olives. Allow to simmer, stirring occasionally roughly 15 minutes, until the mixture thickens.

3. Return drained pasta to the pot. Pour in the tomato mixture, gently toss to combine. Add a little water, if necessary to thin it out.

4. Season to taste with salt and pepper. Top with feta cheese.

Chicken Pasta Salad

A light lunch or dinner in a bowl filled with flavor. Simply change your dressing for a completely different taste!

Serves: 6

Time: 1 hr.

Ingredients:

- rotini pasta (1-1/2 cups, whole grain)
- 1 cup cooked chopped chicken

- 2 cups broccoli florets
- red bell pepper (1/2, chopped)
- green bell pepper (1/2, chopped)
- 1/2 cup finely chopped red onion
- 3/4 cup light Italian salad dressing
- Salt and ground pepper (to taste)

Directions:

1. Prepare the pasta according to manufacturer's instructions. Drain and place in a suitable size bowl.

2. Add the chicken, broccoli, bell pepper, onion and salad dressing. Toss to combine.

3. Season to taste with pepper and salt and toss again.

4. Refrigerate for 30 minutes or until well chilled.

Buffalo Chicken Pizza

Light and tasty pizza your whole family will enjoy.

Serves: 6

Time: 25 mins.

Ingredients:

- 1 package (10 ounces) pre-baked whole wheat thin Italian pizza crust (12-inch)
- 1/4 cup fat-free Ranch dressing
- 1/2 cup finely chopped celery
- 1 cup chopped rotisserie chicken

- 3 tablespoons Buffalo wing sauce
- 3/4 cup red and green bell pepper strips
- 3/4 cup (3 ounces) shredded reduced-fat mozzarella cheese
- 1 tablespoon crumbled blue cheese

Directions:

1. Heat oven to 400°F.

2. Place the pizza crust on an ungreased cookie sheet. Spread the Ranch dressing evenly over the crust. Sprinkle with celery.

3. In a small bowl, stir together the chicken and Buffalo wing sauce. Distribute evenly over the crust. Top with bell pepper strips. Sprinkle with the mozzarella and blue cheeses.

4. Bake until the mozzarella cheese is melted and turning golden, about 10 minutes.

5. Remove from oven and cut into 6 or 12 wedges.

Chicken Strawberry Salad

A simple and delicious way to utilize leftover rotisserie chicken, this fruity salad will become an instant favorite for lunch or dinner.

Serves: 6

Time: 10 mins.

Ingredients:

- rotisserie chicken (2 cups, chopped)
- strawberries (1 cup, sliced)

- reduced-fat feta cheese (1/3 cup)
- mandarin oranges in light syrup (1# 11 ounces can, drained)
- baby spinach (1# 6 ounces package)
- ground black pepper and salt (to taste)
- 1/4 cup fat-free poppyseed dressing
- 6 tablespoons honey-roasted sliced almonds

Directions:

1. Combine the chicken, strawberries, feta cheese, mandarin oranges and spinach in a large bowl.

2. Sprinkle with pepper and salt and drizzle with dressing.

3. Toss well to coat.

4. Share in 6 individual the plates and top each salad with 1 tablespoon almond.

Chunky Chicken Pasta Soup

A quick hearty one pot meal that is easy to prepare and very satisfying. Add crusty whole grain bread and a green salad to complete your meal.

Serves: 8

Time: 50 mins.

Ingredients:

- 1 tablespoon olive oil
- 1 cup chopped onion
- 1 cup chopped green bell pepper
- 1 cup chopped carrot
- 2 cloves garlic, finely chopped
- 2 cans (14-1/2 ounces each) low-sodium chicken broth
- 1 can (14-1/2 ounces) diced tomatoes, undrained
- kidney beans (1# 14 -16 ounces can, rinsed and drained)
- 1 cup diced rotisserie chicken
- 1/2 teaspoon dried basil
- 1/2 cup uncooked small pasta shells
- 1/4 cup shredded Parmesan cheese, for serving, optional

Directions:

1. Heat the oil in a Dutch oven or soup pot over medium-high heat.

2. Add the onions, bell pepper, carrots and garlic and cook, stirring frequently until the vegetables are beginning to soften, 3 to 4 minutes.

3. Stir in the broth, tomatoes, beans, chicken and basil.

4. Bring to the boil on medium-low flame, then lower heat. Simmer, stirring occasionally for 10 minutes.

5. Stir in the pasta and cook, stirring occasionally, until the pasta is tender, 6 to 10 minutes more.

6. Top each serving of soup with 1 tablespoon cheese, if desired.

Edamame Salad with Pork

A fresh and delicious Asian-inspired salad, very easy to prepare. You can have it for a light lunch or dinner.

Serves: 2

Time: 40 minutes

Ingredients:

- 8 ounces frozen shelled edamame
- 1 large naval orange
- 2 tablespoons seasoned rice vinegar
- 1 teaspoon olive oil

- 2 tablespoons chopped green onion
- 6 radishes, thinly sliced
- 1/2 medium cucumber, peeled, seeded and thinly sliced
- 1 cup shredded rotisserie pork

Directions:

1. Cook edamame according to manufacturer's instructions. Drain, then wash off with cold water to stop the cooking process, and pat dry.

2. Grate 1/2 teaspoon orange zest into a large bowl, set aside. Peel the orange and remove the white pith. Slice the orange into rounds and then cut the rounds into quarters.

3. Add vinegar, oil and green onions to the bowl with the zest. Whisk to blend.

4. Add the edamame, radishes, cucumber, pork and orange pieces. Toss to combine and coat with dressing.

BBQ Chicken Pizza

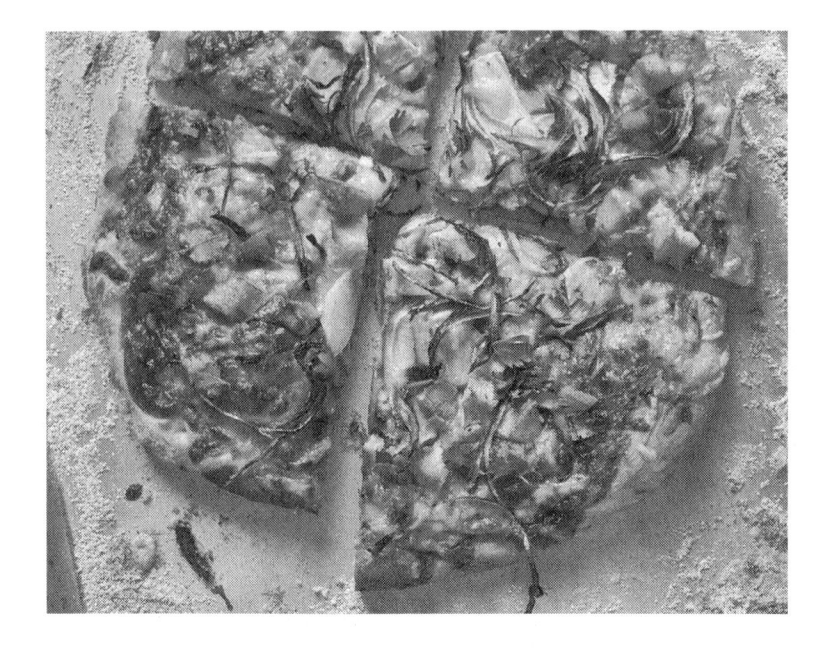

This pizza is fun, and easy to whip up, while being healthy.

Servings: 1

Time: 20 minutes

Ingredients:

- 1 (8-inch) whole wheat low-fat tortilla
- 2 tablespoons barbecue sauce
- 1/2 cup shredded reduced-fat cheddar cheese
- 2/3 cup chopped rotisserie chicken

- 1/2 cup chopped red onion
- 1-1/2 teaspoons chopped fresh cilantro

Directions:

1. Preheat oven to 400°F.

2. Line a baking sheet with foil. Place the tortilla on the foil and bake until crisp, about 4 minutes per side. If air bubbles form, poke them with a fork and then flatten with a spatula.

3. Switch of the oven then top with barbecue sauce. Top evenly with the cheese, chicken, onion and cilantro.

4. Set to bake for about 5 minutes (cheese should melt).

5. Remove from the oven and cut into wedges.

Asian Chicken Noodle Soup

Here we have a quick and easy Asian-inspired chicken noodle soup that's easy, healthy and delicious.

Serves: 4

Time: 30 minutes

Ingredients:

- Water, 3 cups
- ramen noodle soup mix, chicken-flavor, 3 oz.
- chicken, 2 cups, cooked, chopped
- 2 small heads baby bok choy, roughly chopped

- carrot, 1 medium, sliced
- sesame oil, 1 tsp., optional

Directions:

1. Set your water on to boil.

2. Break up the block of noodles. Add the noodles, chicken, bok choy and carrot and stir to combine.

3. Allow to boil and switch the heat to low then simmer gently, uncovered, for 3 minutes, stirring occasionally.

4. Stir in the contents of the noodle seasoning packet and sesame oil, if using.

Chicken Waldorf Salad

This Chicken Waldorf Salad is Creamy, crunchy, sweet and savory, this easy, healthy, and delicious.

Serves: 4

Time: 20 minutes

Ingredients:

- 2 apples, cored and diced
- 1 tablespoon fresh lime juice
- 2 cups diced cooked skinless chicken

- 1/4 cup walnuts, coarsely chopped
- 1/4 cup nonfat plain Greek yogurt
- 1 tablespoon reduced fat mayonnaise
- 2 teaspoons Dijon mustard
- Salt and pepper, to taste
- 8 cups chopped salad greens

Directions:

1. Combine your lime juice and apples.

2. Add the chicken, walnuts, yogurt, mayonnaise, mustard, salt and pepper. Stir to combine.

3. Place two cups of salad greens on each plate. Evenly divide the chicken salad among the 4 plates of greens.

Ranch Chicken Pasta

A creamy, kid-friendly one-dish meal the whole family will love.

Serves: 6

Time: 25 minutes

Ingredients:

- 3 cups uncooked medium no-yolk egg noodles
- 1 tablespoon light butter

- 12 ounces fresh broccoli florets
- Cooking spray
- 2 cups chopped, rotisserie chicken
- 1 cup nonfat buttermilk
- 1/2 cup reduced fat sour cream
- 2 tablespoons dry ranch dressing
- 6 tablespoons cooked real bacon pieces
- 1/4 cup shredded fresh Parmesan cheese
- Freshly ground black pepper to taste

Directions:

1. Set your noodles on to cook until al dente then drain.

2. Add the butter and stir to combine. Keep warm.

3. Microwave the broccoli according the package directions and drain. Then microwave the chicken gently to heat it.

4. Combine your ranch dressing, sour cream, and buttermilk then whisk until smooth.

5. Add the noodles, broccoli and chicken. Toss until evenly coated.

6. If desired, cover and microwave on medium power until gently heated through, 1 to 2 minutes.

7. Sprinkle with bacon, cheese and freshly ground black pepper to taste. Enjoy!

Fiesta Chicken Lasagna

A fun, fresh and zesty family-friendly twist on traditional lasagna.

Serves: 8

Time: 1 hr. 20 minutes

Ingredients:

- 3-1/2 cups thick-and-chunky salsa
- 9 uncooked lasagna noodles
- 2 cups shredded, rotisserie chicken
- black beans, 15oz. drained

- 1/4 cup chopped, fresh cilantro
- 2 cups (8 ounces) shredded, reduced fat Monterey Jack cheese

Directions:

1. Heat the oven to 375°F.

2. Spread ¼ cup of your salsa in the bottom of an ungreased 9 x 13 baking dish.

3. Create layers with 3 sheets of noodles, plus 1/3 of your cheese, salsa, cilantro, black beans, and chicken. Repeat layers two more times.

4. Cover with foil and set to bake for about 40 minutes.

5. Bake uncovered for about 15 more minutes (should be hot in the center).

6. Switch of the oven and allow to rest for about 10 minutes before serving.

Conclusion

Congrats on cooking your way through all 30 rotisserie recipes that are healthy, easy, and delicious. The next step from here would be to continue practicing. With every single steam recipe, you create you will see magic being created.

After you have accomplished that, come on back over and find another amazing journey to partake in from cuisines across the globe in another one of our books. We hope to see you again soon.

Happy cooking!

Made in the USA
Columbia, SC
30 October 2024